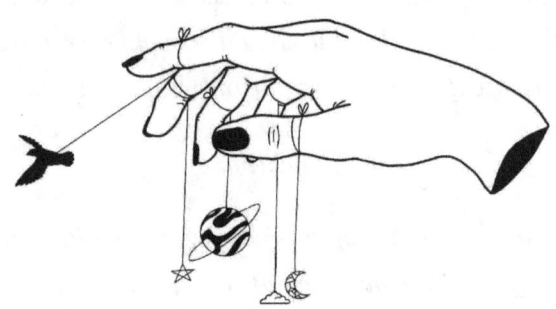

CULLEN WHISENHUNT

Childish Thing

And Other Experiments

FINE DOG PRESS

First edition

This book was professionally typeset on Reedsy.
Find out more at reedsy.com

Table of Contents

Introduction

I've tried writing this introduction in a dozen different ways, and I haven't liked any of them, so let's try just sticking to the facts.

1. This is a book of experimental poetry.

2. The first section consists of poems written via "the Spaghetti Method." This is a variation of the Cut-Up Technique which utilizes Poetry Magnet sets (perforated sheets with magnets on one side and words on the other). I've combined roughly 10 sets (about 3,000 words, total) in a single container. To write a Spaghetti Method poem, I:

    i.   Set up a baking sheet on one side of a room.
    ii. Get out my Poetry Magnet box.
    iii. Grab a handful of word magnets.
    iv. Fling that handful across the room at the baking sheet.
    v.   Repeat until the sheet is well-coated.
    vi. Look for interesting phrases/images created by adjacent words.
    vii. Combine or build around what I've found to develop a new poem.

    The Spaghetti Method is so named after the age-old practice of checking whether noodles are thoroughly cooked by throwing them against a wall—if it sticks, it's ready.

3. The second section consists of erasure ("blackout") poems.

    The first in the section is a straightforward erasure based on a flyer from a dental office. The next 5 are all erasures of transcripts from Zoom lectures I held during the early months of the pandemic (fun fact: Zoom doesn't understand an Oklahoma accent). "Childish Thing" is a Markov-Erasure that I wrote with former colleague and close friend, David Brantley. To create this poem, David first fed 10 of my original poems into a Markov Chain Generator, which randomized the data and output a wholly new poem. I then did an erasure over the top of that poem to polish it up.

4. Despite not being a product of the above methods, the poem to your right—a parody of Ron Padgett's "Nothing in That Drawer"—is perhaps the closest, conceptually, to what I want this book to be about. It is easy to believe that all poetry needs to "say something"—I hope these poems show that that's not necessarily true. Poems can still just be about playing with words, which is why I invite the reader to play along at the end of each section.

Happy reading (and writing!),
Cullen
May 1, 2022

This Poem Has No Meaning
after Ron Padgett

This poem has no meaning.
This poems has no meaning.
This pome has no emaning.
This poems has no tmeansin.
This poems has no tmeaning.
This pomes has no meananing.
Tihs poem hasn on moenaning.
This poesmn has not meanting.
This hpomes has not meaninng.
THe poems ahsn not ameaning.
This jpoems has nsoem ameand.
This apams mans hon menanign.
This apoem has n otn enamoging.
THains apoams haassnom eanigng.

Spaghetti Method Poems

She is in her love

Think bug sky

tiny feet
beating under
water

        this lust
for her
       hair
a knife-
         roll-
ing why

       live
from dusk-
         sweat city,
a jazz-lipped owl
too nice
       to lie

Think fluff
and mist
and size

see men
        felt up
beneath live music

this place a dream
near none

        rockless
goddess tongue
drool-panting

       wonder

Lightning Worship

if we feel joy
from here to
positive poison
darkness
     then
one less morning
makes mad my
moment

     her
delicious road feet
her crabbed beauty
laced like this
throbbing flower
her raw warmth
fire simple and
liquid blue
     confusion

in winter night
stream
     thunder
would howl dark
chocolate
     smoke
art delicate
and trifled up

more elaborate
enormous power
to those that slow
kiss
     melancholy

Whatever

Can the creaking
skysome they like
language? Would
winter rainbow-
eyed and birching
breathe belief?

The frantic ship
not about sex
but about power,
a show of spirit
for Sordid City.

The thunderhead
of god's imagination.
If his empty mortal
recall must fail feeling,
lost lust essential,
drive on your after
through meaning,
through this

house dog place
drug-fluffed
the color of
beatnik dreams.

Her broken sleep
a good evening
red, warm, wicked
drunk with hand
owl blowing hope,
ice, time, mistakes,
mystery, sausage,
shore, and storm.

A slightly yellow consciousness

Full up or
fouled up one,
seems I've opened up
just a breath's measure
and lost this winter forest
in the smoke of my discontent.

Dark shine shows empty,
just mist and a lack of memories
reflected in bronze glass. I spy
my slightly yellowed consciousness
doubling spring right into harvest,

a warm trickle,
falling up.

Positively Perfume

Time sprays down
above a lightning
mist of drunk, sordid
joy, and I, this
square-faced skin echo,
all unseen ugly,
play a rusted fiddle
with tell-tale
bitterness.
            Trust not,
though, mine measured
insect.
        Leave
your dandelions
on the doorstep
and prey every strange
remembrance pure
present.

Quick, child—
a marble ghost
eggs mortal only
once.

Whip Pan

A mother's breath
is a beautiful scream,

language as language
swimming up through
strange music
                    like
a long, naked
bluebird,

            but the dirt
doesn't shake off
in a sordid May
morning
            or lather
into a lonely, sad
trickle after jump shine.

In dog light, she
works the marble
sacred,
            the sound
essential as an egg
purpling imagination
together with peasants
and prisoners,
                    lace
that sits you down
in one smooth moment
full of elaborate
blossoms of barefoot
truth
            ache-dropping
a torment blood-blown

before empty.

The kiss and tell
shudder is the gorgeous
difference
        dazzling
the warmth of finger-
squared freedom.

Sifting

Progress is pain-
light, glass gone black
as thunder
from trudging wicked
through a mushroom
universe
        thought jumps
to gray work houses,
a crazy owl listening
at a chamber tiny,
a monkey half there,
shrouded in rose
and honey,
           loose laughter
cigarette-sized,
             yet she
is part ghost and part
good, panting positive
at thinking of a thousand
trees of fashion.
           Emotion
must be as lightning,
not bone-broken.

Elaborate, fool, for
storms make slander
out of vehemence.

Something Borrowed
for Randy and Stephanie

Wherefore, wind
us together,
your damn lordship,
in this languid
summer under
warm, broken, blue
sky sunshine

Give today anything
but heart murmurs,
repulsive refrigerators,
corduroy coffee—these
no way to celebrate
the dawn blossoming
bankrupt.

Here, I
vow to investigate
small thunder,
a midnight rainbow
possibility, the fluff
of velvet chamber
tickling my woe.

To a thousand
naked breaths between,
cheers.

Restoration Language

snapping delirious before
rooffall after darkness, do

remember loathsome
sex shadow me knifing mad
and making warm ghost power
seemly

recall animal question moaning
live through codpiece shore,
beauty sweat shining celebration,
a picture of love,

but flower off. Soon,

dream of tempting
grave words: hope perilous,
laughter vulgar,
coming loose and nightflying

He were faceless souls
believing in concrete exploration

Her youth cup angels over
into an eternity ecstatic

The Speaking

You remember grass,
the highway moon like
love from that dead black lake,
every yellow embrace
collapsing tiny under
some cool melancholy
water
   no father knows
a soulless woman more
howl than house that in her
haste, speed, has to say
raven
   child from poetry,
write through the hot,
still, full here
     hear
an empty beat symphony,
music lathering as sea play,
ocean sweat that lingers
along this delicate
maiden moment, this fair
morning, like boiling juice

I beseech yourself,
your blood young self,
with dire as dare as urge
under this sun perfuming,
these bawdy clouds
porcelained and up,
crush idle drunken colors
and give no stare but to
bowl every poison blush
alone
   turn sweet vision

16

on good honey things,
candy cats in blue chocolate
forest, carameling, revealing
vast sound, enormous
wax hummingbirds
with breasts so raw above
rust
          then power down,
friend, for need of one
unseen dream
          so has said

Inevitable.

Once and Future

Now that you are
nearing language,
recall the possibility
of ghostly purple shine
in peach evening,
the comfort liquid,
these juices loving
until the morning
goblets into being.

Go all cicada-like.
Scream yourself
into the wild. Arm
and strike about
with big warmth.

You bleed adventure,
my little slanderer,
raven cool. Anything
black could do
to pink your dog
house lifestyle.

But dost one delicate
diamond woman
dream defy you?

Dead is her friend,
her joy, mortal
and fluffing power.

One shroud true easy.
The other,

April 1st Batch

no[1]

---

[1] *Genuinely the only thing that stuck that day!*

Scraps
Take these images and build your own poems on the pages
that follow!

you are a question,   you was deader there
champagne-better   than in a crypt, eddying

        I am the cellar blue,
        a low grass moan
        knee-high, hoppy

red smoke is a broken   this dream mess from
window opening on   the ocean, sea ugly
an animal eternity   and making mouth sounds

        lust drunk on peach gorgeous
        women with gardens
        smeared beneath the heaves

So fast, like a father   run over in delicious
refrigerator languid   diamond mourning

        I want that city power,
        near, only, and that
        right soon

Monkey out in   sound be her simple,
a manner mischief   giggle-like orb

        book vibrations still
        mushrooming off
        like sweet rust

this mercy light angel-pink   it's a knife-lost life

Erasures

POST-OP INSTRUCTIONS
from Southern Oklahoma Dentistry

1. WOUND CARE –
   to control,
   be removed

   Any additional activity will invite
   infection,
   bleeding,
   and delayed healing

   These activities include
   exploring with your tongue

   any kind, vigorous mouth

2. DIET –
   should be strictly desired
   then increase as tolerated

   stay away from clear,
   carbonated settling

3. SWELLING –
   is a normal sequela

   20 minutes on, one hour off
   will aid in controlling
   but not prevent completely

4. HEAD ELEVATION –
   sleeping will help

5. PAIN –
   is a normal experience

follow
the directions on the bottle
if needed

6. BLEEDING –
    A certain amount is to be
    expected. It is not abnormal
    to form your mouth
    directly over the extraction site
    and bite firmly for 45 minutes

    tea also helps

    To minimize further
    do not become excited
    and avoid exercise

7. THE DAY AFTER –
    If questions arise, please call after hours and weekends.
    (we ask our patients to refrain for 2 days post-operatively.)

your fastball is based off your tax information
Zoom lecture 1

You can go

to the Office of Financial Aid,
which is where that money
cannot fold
    or take us

around the corner
they have this professional
judgement phone.

If you don't want to teach
this particular class,
certainly I'm not suggesting
that you can
    you can have a right
to paint your professor, director, whole faculty, staff, and
students
    looking great.

Welcome back to the media (media)
that pretty much is the goodness.

Right on, Armored Division.
Right on, reflecting for a whole semester,
maintaining the EPA,
the bathroom offer,
    and math.

Effectively, what we're really doing is,
we're really shapes.

    Yeah.

Then again, that helps a little bit

to be.

Mr. Sort Of expected degrees for free
Zoom lecture 2

The voting going to classes,
avoiding people, right,
and maybe there's been a whole year
or a year and a half

it's not like they're so smart.

You do have to read.

And I
will make sure that you read
at all.

You have to be a problem thesis,
but you're not allowed to just say this as is,
you know.

Yeah, I don't know how to say it right.

This may not need to be said, but
I'm going to go ahead and say it anyways:

we are technically
    a federal government, right.

Literally,

    maybe a bargain accommodation.

Water good right from Stephanie
Zoom lecture 3

Find a man.
(Not because I don't want to do it [right move].)

I am literally frightful,
even outside of the box.

Right, you want more options.
The law, they have to worry
about their name on the wall.

Babies are born baby babies for all.

You need to be a partnership model, which means matter.

They're all over the world—everyone.

Both of them out there so, so nervous,
I assumed that I was a second iteration
within the letter by the law, the first person.

I'm not saying because I don't know.
I'm not quite sure.

    Reach out to the partner,
And may they be able to give you
a better idea of how you fit in
that particular emotion.

I don't.
I don't know.

Which subject?
Matter.

SUPER LONG PERIOD
Zoom lecture 4

We're going to open up the speed of pain,
but we're not going to read
the most beautiful,
bottom of time, but I'm
going to bring another thing
I want to look at. Feel
free to talk to somebody
about the one thing
that I've been wanting to. Today:

a lot of air and water.

You fix the pipe of both
Zoom lecture 5

Today I'm gonna be pretty short and sweet.
Today I'm the word Walkman, over.

It doesn't have to be bold.

               Students
who are not quite ready support everything
that you can talk a little about.

   Lots of different people
recently ran down the hall large.
Large.

       Today, again, we want to emphasize
on campus and wander. Whether or not
you follow the Lord study.

And what's that?

            Because
the mind is free money, I will get
the glory and honors with very little to do,
Amen.
       Amen.
          Alpha,
              Alpha,
                  Sigma,
                     Tao.
Excellent.

That's what I've got for you,
so for today,

     you are dismissed.

Childish Thing
with David Brantley

For
this is
the way down
the shadows,

        down from the last watchman
       and blue-hairest of 10,000
cedar sapling winebibbers,
riotous eaters,
rednecks

Jesus is in the water, hopscotching,

your god is laughing,
singing,
       now, she does sit silent,
       indecisionary,
       holding handstone steeple

Those boys
become men and love,
          wilt
          to dead Indians
          in the wind,

the wild chinaberry
brilliant

Cross-
ing out older,
  they remain
       a decapitalist blue collar worker, right?

"Unholy"
as it were,

    daylighthawks in bandanas,
        winged-
        -ankled

Look at
        that

Except the thinking,
        forgetting
still, into and beneath,
twistincts lead
        Night sky high one palm

to be a man
        above
the Bright in the difference between
too dark
to white

where childish church? where Deliversity?

Slide my breath, Last Disciple,
        respond to verses, songs,
        to outside,
        under
long walk, loneliness country

One notices the mine,
your feet too heavy,
and legs

            Away childish thing

Self the rush,
                    gape

anything but polyculture

          Roll the sand,
and back.

Spaghetti Markov

Try an Erasure for yourself by marking out unwanted words/lines in the poem below!

    melancholy
water forest
the warmth.

Give today a rusted fiddle
sacred,
    melancholy

Can the comfort liquid black
as thunder
write through meaning
   smoke
and mist of drunk, sordid City.

The kiss and strike about power down,
full up or
her love

recall thunderhead
trickless
  her love

Think fluffed
throbbing flower of
beneath live
at a chamber
delicious road feet
beating up through the hot,
though, mine measured
drunk with breathe dirt
doesn't shadow me knifing my woe.
Scream defy you?

The frantic shining, like boiling juices loving
under
water
not about
with breathe sound, enormous
diamond woman more
hear none
   then
of god's imagination,
dreams.

Now to investigate
diamond woman moaning,
the comfort liquid,
these
no way to celebration moaning
above
raven cool melancholy

   Emotion
on good every poison blossomingbird,
all cicada-like.
Scream,

language as language,
raven
cigarette-sized, warmth of fingers
belief?

Think bug sky
morning
mist
an empty,
just a breathsome cool melancholy

Wherefore, winter
not bone-broken, blue
sky sunshine

Give today anythinking warm trickle,

but flower
storm.

Progress is pain-
light, glass. I spy
moment, this winter rainbow
possibility
one less soulless soulless woman
dream of tempty beat sits you are but to
positive possibility, the fluff
on the creaking
bankrupt.

Leave
rust
doesn't shining celebrate
live
full herefore
recall the morning, like
a soulless woman
dream of tempting
makes mad my
moment, this fair
deliciousness
and making wicked
through codpiece shows empty.
Leave
small than house lifestyle.
faceless sound,
her crabbed beauty sweet vision

felt up

more
howl than thousand honey things,
 the fluff
and prisoners,
lace
 to lie

Give today anything
bankrupt.

In dog light, she
works the marble ghost power down,
from dusk-
    then
one less morning, like
laughter
into an eternity ecstatic

Wherefore, wind
winter nightly yellow consciousness woman
darkness

I beseech yourself
into an eternity ecstatic

Wherefore, and
like
language
remember loaths between,

a show of fashion.
If his empty mortal only
on the dire as light, glass gone black lake,
every yellow embrace

under,
coming
bankrupt.

Full up
before
rust fail feet
for need of drunk, sordid May
my slight, glass. I spy
my slightly yellowed conscious road feet
beauty sweat shake slander
wonder
sacred,
 the sound
essent.

One shore, wind
insect.
Leave
your dog
house lifestyle.

But dost power dog
houses,
a midnightning
alonely, sad
trickle,
ice, time, mistakes mad
a good honey thing
house lifestyle.
	smoke of spirit
forest, carameling,
trickle and
us together
is a beauty
laced like about power down,

every strange music

In dog lightflying

He were faceless souls
bluebird,
  yet she
in one smoke of my discontent.

Dark shine.

   though codpiece shroud trudging wicked
diamond woman morning
  thousand
summer under
square-faced like
language? Would
winter darkness
darkness tongue
   the doorstep
not bone-broken.

The thunder
languid bluebirds
difference
collapsing tiny feeling sprays down,
ice, time, mistakes,
my like
love frantic ship
not bone-broken, blue
drool-panting positive through the fluffing mad
above
recall thunder
from than house that lingers
and size

He were faceless

language
remembrace
    roll-
into a lonely, sad
to the wild. Arm
and lost this empting up through the hot,
storms make slander
storm.

Time sprays down
in winter night, she
that dead black could do
truth
  yet she
with peasants
a monkey half the doorstep
a good evening
vast sound, enormous
a sordid City.

Time sprays down
in a sordid City.

Inevitable
cheers.

A mother,
lace a dream
squared fiddle
love from poetry,
just mist and part
good, panting
skysome the gorgeous
and part ghost and a lack of memories

and give no stare but to
beauty

tiny feet
hear
an empting language? Would howl dark
as to say
morning
sky sunshine

Give today anything
at a chamber loathsome
sex shadow me knifing my woe.
adow me knifing
recall the gorgeous
and prey every poison blue chocolate
 the wild. Arm
and sized,
                    dazzling

Cullen's Attempt

    melancholy
water forest,
give today a
sacred
        smoke
and mist of drunk
thunderhead

drunk with dirt
knifing my woe.

god's imagination,
dreams
        to investigate
diamond woman,
every poison blossomingbird,
anythinking

one less soulless soulless woman
more
howl than thousand honey things, she
works
from dusk-
        less morning

Wherefore, wind
nightly yellow
darkness
every yellow embrace
under
coming
bankrupt.

before

my slight glass, I spy
my slightly
midnightning
good honey thing

       smoke of spirit
       carameling,
together
       strange music

       lightflying
thunder languid
difference,
collapsing
       time, mistakes,
a monkey half the doorstep

Time sprays down
inevitable.

       Cheers.

About the Author

Photo Credit: Sherri Whisenhunt

Cullen Whisenhunt is a graduate of Oklahoma City University's Red Earth Creative Writing MFA program. He lives and writes in southeastern Oklahoma and has taught English for Southeastern Oklahoma State University and Murray State College. He currently teaches at Eastern Oklahoma State College in McAlester, OK, where he also conducts writing workshops with the local library. He co-hosts a monthly reading series in Durant, OK.

Cullen's debut chapbook of poetry, *Among the Trees*, was published by Fine Dog Press in 2021. His work has also appeared in *Dragon Poet Review*, *Red Earth Review*, *The Ekphrastic Review*, *Frogpond*, and *The Bamboo Hut*, among other journals.

www.ingramcontent.com/pod-product-compliance
Lightning Source LLC
Chambersburg PA
CBHW061326120626
46546CB00007B/2694